Z⁰⁰

D0824596

Best wishes —

Kip Taylor 1991

LOON

Dedication

To my wife, Shar, for keeping film in my cameras and food over my campfires, and for sharing an elusive dream for so many years.

LOON

Photographed and written by **Kip Taylor**

Publisher

LOON published by
Kip Taylor
P.O. Box 23
Saranac Lake, New York
12983

Production

Book Art, Inc.
302 Bridgeland Avenue
Toronto, Ontario
Canada M6A1Z4
Manager: Benjamin KOO

Typography

Coneco Laser Graphics, Inc.
58 Dix Avenue
P.O. Box 3255
Glens Falls, New York
12801

Typography consultants

Dennis Brower
David Stewart

Layout and Design

Kip Taylor

Copyright

Copyright 1988 by Kip Taylor
Reproduction in any manner in whole or in
part, in English or in other languages, is
prohibited. All rights reserved

Library of Congress catalogue card number 87–090324

ISBN 0-9623422-0-3

Printed in Hong Kong

Contents

Introduction: Shots Never Fired

I was once hired by a television network to film certain events of a prestigious horse show. Apparently the reason for the job offer was to get file footage on some of the riders who would be competing in the Olympic Games the following year. As in most free-lance assignments, details were all worked out over the telephone. The technical director recited a long list of competitors and indicated at what part of the course he wanted them filmed. Every so often the "brick wall jump" was mentioned and I dutifully wrote everything down in my film log book.

The following day I visited the horse show grounds and was given a tour of the course. Everything looked as the director had indicated it would except for one thing. There was no "brick wall jump." A bit disturbed, I called New York and explained the situation to him. His answer was curt. "For crying out loud! Don't tell me what you *can't* get . . . send me what you *can* get!" That unsympathetic answer has since taken on an intelligent meaning: Get what you can . . . that's all that's expected of you.

I have tried to adapt this motto to my nature photography. It is sometimes strained. One morning, I was checking out loon nesting activity in a large cattail marsh when I heard the unmistakable sound of a deer slowly wading. Excited about getting a bonus shot or two, I paddled and pushed my canoe through shoulder-high corridors of reeds and cattails toward the sound. My movie camera was loaded, ready and within easy reach. The sound was very close. One more paddle shove sent me into a patch of fairly open water and . . . face to face with a huge black bear sow! She was stomach-deep in swamp water, water lily leaves and stems hanging out of both sides of her muzzle. Behind her, a chubby cub sat on the shore, while a second youngster clung to a tree about six feet above the ground.

When I mentioned the incident to a friend a few weeks later, he exclaimed, "WOW! You must have gotten some fantastic footage!" At the time the only "footage" I was interested in was the amount of it between me and the mother bear, that animal which experienced woodsmen feel is the most dangerous on the North American continent. To make matters worse, I had to BACK out of that green labyrinth! My camera was still loaded and ready, just where I had left it.

This is only one of many incidents that illustrates the fact that nature photography is far from being an exact science. So many factors are involved. Lighting, weather, equipment, logistics, and especially the subject can cause gray hairs. When people ask me how someone becomes a professional photographer, my stock answer is "Buy a tripod." It's true. So often those hand-held shots end up on the cutting room floor or are sent back as unselected slides by knowledgeable photo editors. Of course this rule is often broken. Loons usually perform their mating displays out in the middle of their lake or pond. In those situations you hand-hold and pray a lot. A canoe is not tripod country.

Trying to outguess nature and its creatures is a full-time job for wildlife photographers. We're usually wrong. One afternoon in late May, I was fortunate enough to capture on film the construction of a loon nest. After putting the finishing touches on it, the loon pair disappeared around the end of the island. Because the first egg is normally laid the day after the nest is built, I dismantled all my film equipment and loaded the canoe, planning to be back the next morning to film the rare event. I was just about ready to shove off when a movement caught my eye. A single loon came back around the island and went directly to the nest site. Without hesitation she struggled up on the nest, turned around . . . and laid an egg. I watched the whole thing through binoculars!

Equipment is always a factor. Anything with moving parts falls under Murphy's law. Reloading a camera with frozen, fumbling fingers can be an adventure. Having your breath condense on the lens or viewfinder during an exciting moment can cause baldness. Cross-threading a tripod screw is the second leading cause of insanity. The use of long lenses is the LEADING cause. Bird photography almost always has to be done from a distance. Often, as in the case of the skittish loons, the distance can be nearly a half-mile. After fastening one of those huge lenses to a heavy-duty tripod and attaching a camera, the photographer's fun begins. Focusing on a subject halfway across a lake requires the precision of a neurosurgeon. Frequently the field of focus is less than six feet . . . three feet in front of and three feet behind the subject. A quivering movement at the camera is multiplied ten-fold when it reaches the subject.

I was fortunate to have been introduced to the woods and waters very early in life. My parents instilled in me an appreciation of all of nature's treasures. When I entered the film business in 1968, I wanted to find a film subject that had not been done and redone by previous photographers, and also one that was available in my Adirondack area. I chose loons. I guess I'd always had a secret love affair with the loon, which to me is the symbol of the wilderness waters. My initial research revealed that there were only three references on loons in the Library of Congress. The field was certainly wide open. Off and on from 1969 to 1987 I followed the loons in their summer habitat in the Adirondacks. Some years the study was intense. Other years I tried to fill in with pictures I had previously missed.

The contents of this book represent the best of what I photographed in those eighteen years. I shot almost twenty-five thousand feet of movie film. Of the over six thousand slides I have taken of loons, quite a few were discarded as poor quality. Many are still in my files for future use. However, I'm the only one who recalls with a twinge of regret those exciting scenarios I missed: those shots never fired.

1

Loon country

ice-out: arrival

Ice-out: Arrival

For years I believed the loons returned to their Adirondack ponds the same day the ice actually went out. Because I had heard and read this statement several times from fairly reliable sources, I had no reason to doubt its validity . . . until I tried to film the loons' arrival.

To wager on the ice going out of a certain pond on a certain day is comparable to betting on the State Lottery. My loon diary contained dozens of ice-out dates, all different. I had to even the odds. I arranged for several private pilots in the area to monitor specific ponds during routine flights over or near my study area and let me know when ice breakup began. Since we were not content to wait by the telephone, my wife, Shar, and I checked ice conditions on ponds we could reach on foot.

Four days of checking finally paid off. Late one afternoon we stood on the shore of a pond that showed all the telltale signs of impending breakup. House size holes of open water could be seen reflecting the setting sun at the far end. Excited, we headed for home. Later that evening one of the pilots called and verified our findings. I was ready.

The next morning found me back at the pond. A strong wind was blowing. Waves formed and by mid-morning a large stretch of ice-free water allowed me to paddle my canoe to one of the islands. From that vantage point I could watch the entire pond. I waited for the loons . . . and waited. By sundown all traces of ice had disappeared, and still no loons had arrived. Racing darkness, I loaded the canoe and headed for the mainland.

I was back on the island before the sun came up the following morning. As soon as it was light enough, I set up my camera equipment and scanned the pond surface through a large telephoto lens. Still no loons! I double checked the camera gear and waited. The rising sun cast a pink glow that slowly took on a yellow hue as it climbed higher in the morning sky. Suddenly, a distant movement just above the horizon caught my eye. Peering through the telephoto lens, I focused on the tiny speck. There was no mistake. It was a loon. Just clearing the trees, it set its wings, executed a long downward glide, and landed at the far end of the pond. Although a day late, the first loon had arrived. Others would follow. Winter in the Adirondacks was finally over.

All traces of ice gone, the first loon arrives on its pond. Loons may migrate singly, in pairs or in small flocks. It is believed that the males of the species arrive first to reclaim their territorial waters.

Typical loon behavior is absent the first few hours following arrival. Little preening, calling or even diving is seen. Slow cruising seems to be the only activity as the bird quietly establishes boundary lines. In the early spring territories are not defended. Transient birds are usually allowed on others' home waters, a necessary concession since their own ponds could still be ice bound.

It is late afternoon when the second loon arrives and joins its mate.

2

Loon country

close-up

The common loon in its breeding plumage is the most beautiful bird in the world. To describe it as simply black and white doesn't do it justice. When light strikes the head and neck its plumage is a blue-green velvet. The white dots of the necklace and the stripes of the collar stand out in relief against the black of the neck. Blue-black lines run down the lower neck and dissolve into the main body pattern. I like to think God draped the loon's back with an intricate black and white checkered quilt. The breast, chest and abdomen are pure white. Males and females have identical plumage.

The loon's oversized webbed feet, set far back on the body, are nearly useless on land. Loon, a derivative of lumme or lummox, means either one who is clumsy or one who walks with a limp. Yet in the water, its speed and agility have led people to rename it the Great Northern Diver. Any creature that can outswim a fleeing brook trout has to have something extra under the hood!

Unlike most other birds, the loon has nearly solid bones enabling it to attain neutral density in the water. If it weren't for air-filled lungs, a loon could not float. By adjusting the amount of air in its feathers and lungs, a loon can ride in the water at any depth it chooses. Sometimes, almost the entire body is visible; on other occasions only its head is above water. Adult loons generally weigh an average of between nine and thirteen pounds and males are usually larger than females.

We've worked many times trying to time the length of loon dives. With stopwatch in hand, Shar and I need to sit back to back in the canoe to cover the 360 degrees in which the diving loon could surface. Starting the timing is easy. We just press the stopwatch when the loon goes under. Then the search begins. We never know where the loon will resurface, or if it will let its entire body or just its head emerge. We've had to discount many timings when we noticed that the loon was suddenly there, but we hadn't actually seen it come up. In the end, we were able to get enough countable dives to determine that the average dive lasts about ninety seconds. The longest dive we timed was a little over three minutes. Under duress or in extremely deep dives, I'm sure it can stay under longer. There is a theory that loons, along with some other aquatic creatures, are able to regenerate their own oxygen supply.

Another impressive feature of the loon at close range is the blood-red eye. Actually, it is the iris that is colored. The lens is dark brown or black. Of all the loon's senses, vision seems to be the keenest. A unique problem exists concerning the eyesight of diving birds: the necessity to see underwater as well as above. In my research, I learned that because the focusing effect of the cornea is impaired when submerged, the lens, being soft, can be transformed into a pear shape to improve focus. It may be that the loon can actually see better underwater than in the air. As all birds, loons have nictitating membranes that can cover the eyes. This semi-transparent membrane acts much like a human eyelid to cleanse and lubricate as well as shade the eye. Loons don't blink as we do, but occasionally the membrane will close and reopen. I remember the first time I saw a loon falling asleep on its nest. The membrane slowly moved up to obscure the red eye. Some believe that the membrane is closed during flying and diving.

The hearing ability of the loon is excellent, and it is probably capable of hearing infra-sounds. Because birds have no external ear, we tend to forget that sound plays an important part in their world. A nesting loon seems to be aware of every sound emitted on the pond. I experimented with a loon's response to sounds I made while sitting in my film blind. In one test, it repeatedly looked in my direction whenever I scratched the back of my hand. My blind was twenty-three feet from the nest.

The Eye

Although the eye is located on the side of its head, the loon is able to pivot the eyeball, giving it partial frontal vision: a necessity for catching fish.

The Bill

Strong jaw muscles enable the loon to exert tremendous seizing, holding and pulping pressure. Tiny backward-pointing denticles, located on the tongue and roof of the mouth, aid in positioning and swallowing the food.

The necklace is often confused with the collar, located a few inches below it. As this photograph illustrates, tiny rectangular white feather patches form the necklace pattern.

Collar Markings: Tools of Identification

During the early years of my loon filming, I searched for a method of determining if the same pairs of loons returned to the same ponds each year. At that time, little banding or pair bond research had been done. I worked so closely with one particular pair that I felt confident I recognized them in subsequent years by their looks and actions alone. However this was hardly scientific enough to convince anyone. Resigned to the idea that banding was probably the only method that would allow us to get conclusive results, I applied for, and received, a Federal banding permit as well as all of the bands and literature that came with it. Inquiring about the best way to band loons, I was told that if I found out, I should let them know. While I was waiting for the necessary State banding permit, I thought long and hard about the project. First of all, I had absolutely no experience in banding procedures. The only way I thought I could capture the birds was while they were on the nest, and this presented a great risk to the eggs. Loons are not plentiful enough to endanger even one chick. After considerable agonizing, I decided to drop the idea of trying to band our loons. I had to find another way.

One night, my parents, Shar and I were sitting in the living room watching loon slides, many of which showed close-ups of the loons' collar markings. I could identify the year when they were taken by the pond they were on and the specific location of the nest. As slide followed slide, we suddenly realized that the collar markings were as individual as fingerprints. We became quite excited about this and did considerable sorting and comparing, taking lengthy notes. We were definitely on to something.

Using binoculars for skittish pairs, and film blinds for birds more accustomed to my presence, I drew pictures of the right-side collar markings of five pairs of loons. The next year, I compared the collars of the loons with my art work: At least five pairs of "marked" loons did return to the same Adirondack ponds.

Because of other film commitments the third year, we all but discontinued the program. However, we did continue to monitor one particular pair and proved, at least to ourselves, that they returned and nested for five successive years in the same breeding territory. This sixth year brought us up short. The male loon returned . . . with a new mate! Shar and I could only speculate about the fate of his previous

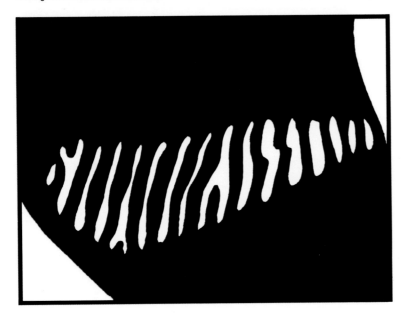

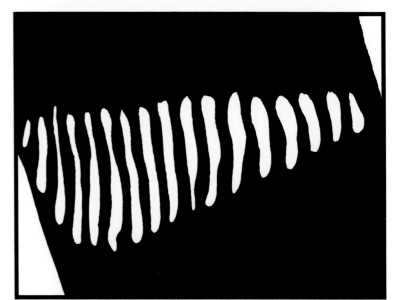

partner. Although saddened by her absence, we did feel quite professional at being able to identify certain loons by their collar markings.

This type of identification in the field is difficult. As a loon turns its head, the tiny feathers that make up the collar pattern become unalined and distort the normal stripes, V's and Y's. I've taken great pains to get drawings and photos of each nesting loon when its head was facing straight forward. Only in comparing slides and drawings can I get a truly accurate identification.

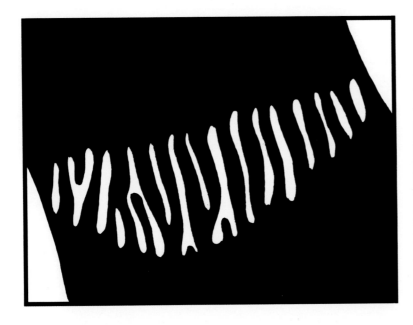

Plumage: The Back

On land the radiant black and white loon contrasts sharply with the muted hues of the shoreline, but on water it achieves a natural camouflage. From above, the checkerboard pattern blends subtly with the dancing light reflections of a choppy pond surface; from below, the loon's white underbody blends into the sky.

The wings of a loon are thick and powerful. Unlike most aquatic birds, loons often use their wings to propel themselves on the water's surface and, on rare occasions, underwater.

The Crown

The feathers on the crown of a loon's head can be raised or lowered, altering the bird's profile. This reflex action, immediately preceding a dive, is the start of the total compression of the bird's entire feather covering. It squeezes out any trapped air that may hinder the submerged loon from achieving neutral buoyancy.

Set well back on the body, the legs and large webbed feet are capable of propelling a submerged loon at speeds exceeding fifteen miles per hour. When a loon is sitting still in the water, its legs hang freely and its feet dangle in a folded position.

3

Loon country

behavior

Behavior

Except when nesting, the loons in the Adirondacks spend their time above, on and below the water of their territorial ponds. To the casual observer loons seem to wile away their summers simply loafing. Actually, the "loafing" loon is nearly always busy. Body maintenance is continuous and necessary for survival. Preening and straightening its feathers almost hourly insures that the loon will remain sleek, clean and waterproof. Anything less than constant attention invites parasites, disease or hypothermia.

On territorial waters relatively undisturbed by human encroachment, loons sleep at irregular intervals during the daylight hours. The sleeping posture seldom varies. The head and neck are folded back over the upper body, and the bill is often holstered under a wing. Although seemingly unconscious to its surroundings and appearing to drift aimlessly, the loon has its alert system switched on signaling its large feet to paddle frequently enough to keep the bird away from shore.

A few years ago I stayed up all one night in my canoe following a loon pair during the hours of darkness. Although I heard some calling, the loons tended to stay in one area and conversation between the pair was minimal. Every so often I turned my flashlight on them, and invariably they would stare back at me. If they slept that night I couldn't catch them in the act!

A curious chink in the behavioral armor of the loon exists, at least here in the Adirondacks. It concerns the defense of its nesting site weeks or even months after the young are hatched. I discovered this unusual trait one cold October day during the seventh year of my study. Attempting to get photos of the adolescent birds flying, I set up my equipment on an island that had been the nest site of the resident loon pair earlier that spring. Not having much luck filming and experiencing considerable discomfort from the cold, I decided to build a small fire. After clearing a spot, I began breaking branches for kindling, and I hadn't been at it for more than a few minutes when a faint noise made me turn around. Thirty or forty feet out in the water sat the loon pair staring at me. A little surprised, I asked the loons how everything was going and how the family was. The loons promptly dove and surfaced way out in the pond. Smiling, I went back to my firebuilding.

I needed some heavier wood so I began breaking some arm-thick branches. I hadn't broken more than half a dozen when a movement caught my eye. Out in the water, even closer than before, sat the loon pair.

My curiosity was aroused. I had spent half the day sitting behind my camera while the adult loons avoided me and fished and preened down at the far end of the pond. Now, after I had built a fire, the loons wouldn't leave me alone. Was it the crackling fire that brought them in so close? If not, what? The breaking of branches? The loons were losing interest and were swimming slowly out into the pond. Grabbing a handful of small branches, I broke them across my knee. The response was immediate. Both loons whirled and swam silently but quickly toward me. So that was it! They were worried about their island. But why? Were the nesting bonds still tied?

Hurriedly checking my campfire, I crashed and broke branches along the shoreline as I moved toward the old nest site. The loons quickly followed. Suddenly both birds broke into tremolos as they rushed toward the grown-up nest site. Talk about old habits dying hard! It had been more than three months since the birds had used the nest and they were still defending it. With as little noise as possible, I went back to my campfire. The loons returned to the center of the pond.

A rare case? Not at all. In the years following my discovery of this quirk in the loons' usual shy behavior, I have repeated the experiment with the same results. Needless to say, any method to bring the loons closer to a camera lens is a boon. I don't mind admitting that I have used this technique as a "parlor trick", especially for close friends. In one instance, I was standing near a former mainland nest site talking with a forest ranger. Noticing a single loon out in the pond he remarked how beautiful the bird was. "Heck, Joe," I said. "You can hardly see the bird from here. Let me call it in so you can get a good, close look." I started crunching and breaking branches and sticks and, as if on cue, the loon sped in toward us, stopping about twenty feet out from the awe-struck ranger. Since that day, I've noticed whenever that forest ranger drives by our house, he tends to speed up a little!

*As if casually hailing a friend, a loon displays
what naturalists have dubbed a
"foot waggle." This behavior, usually seen in
conjunction with preening, is probably nothing more than a stretching maneuver.*

Peering

Immersing the bill and eyes underwater is an unceasing activity. Peering under the pond surface, it can locate food, detect predators and follow the movements of its submerged mate or offspring.

Preening

Nearly floating on its back, a loon meticulously preens its feathers. Using its head as a swab, it oils its body frequently, insuring a water-proof coat. The oil is secreted by the uropygial gland, a small skin sack located at the base of the tail.

Wing Flapping

From a distance the wing flap of a loon is highly visible. Rising slowly to a standing position, the bird vigorously flaps its wings, sending droplets of water in all directions. This behavioral act apparently helps to dry the wings, realign the feathers and stretch the muscles.

Sleeping

4

Eating

The loons residing on Adirondack lakes and ponds are primarily fish eaters. If trout and salmon appear to be their favorite fare, it is only because those particular species are available. Smelt, dace and suckers, either re-introduced by illegal bait-fishing or survivors of incomplete reclamation (poisoning) are probably next on the loon's preference list. The fact that all these species fall into the category of soft or non-coarse fish presents a unique problem to the observer or, in my case, photographer who wants to learn more about the loon's eating habits. Once overtaken and caught, these fish present no swallowing problem, and are usually eaten underwater, on the run so to speak.

Common sense dictates the size of the fish preyed upon by the loon. More than a few people have told me they had observed loons devouring trophy-sized fish, in one case "at least a twenty inch trout." Another swore that "that bass the loon had easily went five pounds!" I guess anything is possible. A few years ago I watched and photographed a loon attempting to swallow what appeared to be a pond sucker measuring about fourteen inches. Even though these birds have the ability to enlarge their gape, much like snakes, this particular loon was literally choking to death, and finally left the oversized fish floating on the pond surface. It then dove in search of smaller prey. Coarse or spiny fish such as bullheads, perch or bass are occasionally brought to the surface to be pulped or mutilated before swallowing is attempted.

Pond vegetation constitutes the next largest segment of the loon's diet. Centuries of organic matter settling to the bottom of our lakes and ponds have created a fertile muck that nurtures entire forests of aquatic plants. The two underwater species that the Adirondack loon seems to prefer are the Leafy Pondweed, *Potamogeton foliosus* and the White Water Lily, *Nymphaea odorata.* Submerged pond vegetation, brought to the surface by the adults, is an important dietary staple for loon chicks during the first six to eight weeks of their lives. Another aquatic plant apparently enjoyed by the loons is the Water Willow, *Decodon verticillatus.* It is interesting to note that the loons only feed upon this plant during the month of June.

Rounding out the loon's diet are crayfish, mussels, frogs, polywogs and sometimes aquatic insects. Through binoculars, I once watched an adult loon bring a large mussel to the surface and masticate it for nearly a minute before swallowing it. Broken shell and all. As for insects, I witnessed a nesting loon pluck a dragon fly out of the air and swallow it without hesitation. This was probably rare, as I do not think that pond insects make up very much of the general diet.

Supplementary Diet

crayfish

pond vegetation

frogs

tadpoles

mussels

pond insects

Drinking

As any creature, loons require drinking water. Not unlike a barnyard fowl, the loon tilts its head back to swallow.

5

Loon country

flying

Flying

It is difficult to discuss loons in flight without describing the sounds that accompany them. The two are inseparable. I don't even have to see it to know that a loon is taking off or winging high overhead at full speed. I can tell by the sound. Unlike ducks which jump off the water into immediate flight, the loons have to work much harder to become airborne, because they are quite large and heavy in relation to their wing size. To take off, the loon literally has to half-run and half-fly across the pond surface into the wind, using both feet and wings to gain speed. Because of this, they require a longer runway than most other waterfowl, a fact which governs the selection of ponds on which to land, fish and nest. I believe that loons would have a difficult time taking off from a pond smaller than twenty acres, although the shape of the pond could vary this. The sound of a loon taking off is a staccato patpatpatpatpat as the wings and feet touch the water leaving a visual pattern of splash marks gradually becoming farther apart as the loon increases speed.

Once the loon clears the water, it gains altitude slowly. Most of the time it circles its own pond at least once before heading on. Maybe it is reinforcing in its mind just how its home looks, but that's speculation on my part. Naturalists estimate that loons travel at fifty to seventy-five miles per hour.

A number of years ago, Shar was with me while I was trying to film loons in flight on slow-motion movies. I'd been describing to her how difficult it was just keeping them in the viewfinder since they moved at such high speeds. She decided she would try her hand with the camera. After a while, we saw a loon circling, getting ready to land on the pond. Shar aimed and fired off the camera while the film whirred through it at twice normal speed to record slow-motion. The loon flew over us from right to left. Shar followed with the camera. I watched both as the loon changed course and circled back while Shar continued to focus on where the loon was originally headed. I thought of the cost of the wasted film whizzing through the camera, and I yelled, "Just what in the heck are you shooting?" Shar stopped the camera and turned around in the canoe to find out why I was so upset. I pointed to where the loon had landed off to our right. Then she admitted that she had lost sight of the loon against the backdrop of the mountain, but had kept filming, trying to maintain the same speed and flight path of the bird until it reappeared. Carefully she handed the camera back to me. I don't think she's touched it since.

There are two sounds that identify loons in full flight. One is the repeated "squeaking" which corresponds to the wing beats. It is unique. Once you've heard it and made the association, you know it's a loon overhead without looking. The other sound is the call made in flight. Though most claim that the call is just a variation of the tremolo used on the water, it is quite distinctive to me. It is like the tremolo sound but repeated over and over at a higher or shriller pitch, with little, if any, inflection. I've never heard loons make exactly that same call on the water. Again, when I hear that, there is no doubt in my mind that the loon is flying.

It's fairly easy to identify a flying loon even if it's not calling. Its body in the air is hunched with the back high, head and neck down and feet trailing off behind. The feet, though not touching, are in a "clap-hands" position, offering little if any wind resistance.

Loon landings are a joy to watch. Each time I see one I am reminded of the old PBY's or Flying Boats that were used in World War II. Again, daring to be different, loons land on their breasts with their feet straight out behind them. As they approach their landing spots the loons set their wings, cupping them slightly toward their bodies. Instead of coming straight down, they use a long runway, and speed across the pond gradually getting lower and lower. If they have brakes, they certainly don't use them because they touch down at top speed sending sprays of water high into the air on both sides. The bow waves they create help to slow them down.

Loons seem to prefer early mornings to do their main flying, and as far as I know they don't fly at night. At least I've never heard the flying call in the darkness. Though I've seen exceptions where a loon will take off quite quickly and without the benefit of a headwind, the norm is a long run into the wind. I don't know how many times I've watched a loon run the entire length of a pond only to swim back and try again.

Take-off

A selection of photographs, taken over many years, is grouped together in an attempt to show loons at various stages of flight.

Full Flight

Landing

6

Loon country

calling

Calling

The call of the common loon is one of the most beautiful sounds in nature. A long drawn out wail drifting across a fog-shrouded, early-morning pond is our assurance that the wilderness sentry is standing guard. Most references concerning loons state that there are four major calls in their repertoire. The first are the wails, sustained notes used to summon their mates or to advise the chicks to stay close. The second call is the tremolo or laughing call used to denote fear or excitement. The third is the yodel, supposedly given only by the male loons. This call is used to warn intruders that they are trespassing. The fourth "call" is really a catch-all category for several loon utterances. Known as the talking or conversation calls, they run the gamut from "hoots" of the adults to "peeps" of the youngster.

During my years of living with and filming loons, I have heard three additional "calls" that warrant attention. One is probably used only about eight hours a year. I first heard this call in 1973, four years after I began my study. It is a soft "meowing" sound possibly uttered only by the female. This call is made while the loon pair is searching for a suitable nest site and preparing to mate. Its tone evokes a feeling of urgency or concern.

The second of these little-known calls is truly unusual. I heard it during the fifth year of my loon study. One extremely tolerant pair allowed me to set my filming blind quite close to their nest. Vegetation that was very low early in the incubation period grew to obstruct my filming vision as the days passed. With a pair of long-handled clippers I snipped my way toward the nesting bird. The loon allowed me to get within three feet of her. Reaching out with the clippers I attempted to trim a clump of grass inches from her. Slowly she stretched her neck forward and touched the jaws of the offending tool while emitting from deep in her throat a loud, growl, much like a dog would make. I was invading her space and she was warning me. I backed off.

The last of these three very special calls is one we were finally able to capture on sound tape after seventeen years. We refer to it as the "clucking" call. It is a sound that somehow would be more appropriate in a barnyard than on a pond for it is chicken-like in quality. The call is used by the adult to summon the chick. It is a difficult sound to describe. Phonetically the call would be written like this: "WUHHHHH, KUH-KUH-KUH-KUH KUH-KUH-KUH." It begins with a "WUH" followed by six or seven staccato "KUH" sounds, the last three at a lower pitch. Starting at medium volume it fades out at the end. Sometimes the first syllable has a tremolo quality. My experience has been that loons use this call for about four weeks following the chick's hatching.

Even though the wail is a "throat" call, it can be heard over long distances.

The Yodel

A unique posture is assumed when a loon yodels. The bill is closed as the loon's throat swells, but is opened for the actual call. Sustained harassment by humans, the presence of predatory birds such as hawks and eagles, and the violation of territorial boundaries by other loons will provoke this call. Small planes, motor boats and sonic booms are apparently considered threatening too, since I've often heard yodels directed at them.

The Tremolo

Tremolos are probably the most commonly used calls in high traffic areas. At the first sign of danger, a loon begins these vocalizations. On many occasions I have been unwittingly assisted by an adult loon as I searched for its nest site. The frequency and intensity of the tremolos reminded me of a children's game, with the loon shouting, "You're getting warm. Now you're getting cold. You're getting warmer. You're getting HOT!"

The vocalizations of loons are being studied with greater intensity than ever before. Not only is its call being analyzed, but its voice is too. Space-age technology, in the form of sonagrams has come to loon country to aid in the identification of specific birds. Calls of loons are recorded, and through a computer, "voice patterns" printed out. As with fingerprints and collars, no two voices are exactly alike, thus giving researchers another tool to help unravel the mystery of the loon.

Loon country

courtship

Courtship

The courtship displays of the loons on Adirondack waters run the gamut from spectacular to dramatic to serene. They are probably unnecessary from a biological point of view. Because loons, like swans and geese, pair bond for life, wooing and winning a mate each spring is usually not a problem. Exceptions may include birds entering their first breeding year. So why do many of these birds expend the time and energy trying to impress their life-long partners? Probably just for the fun of it and for the loons in my study area, mid-May seems to trigger the activity. On nine different ponds nine different loon pairs approach the courtship ritual in their own way.

Spectacular

A few of the paired loons in my study area perform spectacular courtship displays.

Exciting

Excessive vocalizing and vigorous wing rowing characterize the dramatic courtship rituals of some of the loons.

Serene

For the majority of courting loons, nodding, neck-rubbing and bill-dipping are the only actions displayed before mating.

8

Loon country

nesting

Nesting

The early days of June find the Adirondack loon pair searching for a nest area. Usually about two days are spent inspecting possible sites before a final choice is made, and there are many factors that govern the nest location. The availability of nest-building materials, the proximity to the water and the depth of the water are considerations.

Within their selected pond, the loons may have three general areas from which to choose: mainland, islands or wetlands. The selection of a mainland site is usually the poorest choice and only made as a last resort. Because predators such as minks, raccoons, fishers, bobcats, and even bears regularly patrol the wilderness shorelines, a loon nest built along these predation routes stands little chance of survival.

A second and much better choice is an island site, although the size is of some importance. Loons appear to prefer islands of an acre or less, either heavily wooded or containing underbrush. Larger islands tend to harbor a predator population and also invite the encroachment of humans interested in exploring or camping.

The third choice usually yields the most successful nests: in or near a bog or marsh. Here, the threat of human annoyance is greatly reduced. Marshes are not high on the list for most boaters and hikers in the Adirondacks. Frog hunting has all but disappeared in many areas, thus keeping more people out of the wetlands. In marshes, muskrat houses and feeding platforms are often used by loons for nest sites. Additional aquatic vegetation can then be easily dredged up by the loons to complete the nest. The nest must be built high enough so that waves caused by wind or motorboats can not reach the eggs. It has to be situated near water deep enough to allow the setting bird, in an emergency, to easily slide off the nest and quickly submerge to escape.

Probably the most important factor that makes marsh loon nests so successful is a unique swamp security system. We refer to it as the "Swamp Air Force." Its members include redwing blackbirds, rusty blackbirds, kingbirds and tree swallows. These spunky song birds are the eyes and ears as well as the protectors of their territories. It is a brave gull, crow, heron or hawk that enters the airspace above such a marsh. Like tiny fighter planes, dozens of these little birds streak skyward to meet and usually repel the intruder. There is definitely strength in unity.

The loon pair searches for a nest site. The same pair had "false nested" twice in the past few days. They had selected a nest site, started the construction and suddenly abandoned it.

Even loons take shortcuts! The final selection of a nest site is one that had produced a successful hatch two years earlier. Located on the lee side of an island and hidden somewhat from normal view, it is a wise choice.

Unlike the construction of a new nest, little work has to be performed other than pulling a few seedlings and removing unwanted sticks from the nest.

The Egg

The female lays an egg the following afternoon. Although I have never been close enough to see the egg actually emerging, I have watched the procedure from a distance. She pants, raises and lowers her tail and moves her body from side to side as the egg is laid.

Types of Nests

The construction of a loon nest must be an instinctive activity. If the "blueprints" are passed on to the next generation it must be along the genetic chain. The chick or chicks are not even encased in a hard eggshell when most nests are built, so no "on-the-job training" is ever possible there.

Most loon nests are within five feet of the water's edge. Most measure about two feet in diameter and eighteen inches high. All have a saucer-shaped depression in the dome which contains the eggs. The rim of this crater normally prevents the eggs from being accidently rolled out, even when the nesting loon has to depart the nest mound quickly.

Many loon nests are constructed of rotting and soggy pond vegetation raked up from the pond bottom. This is heaped in a loosely layered pile to be compacted by one or both loons using their bodies as "tamping tools." During its first few days the nest is a wet, firm mound facing the sky, a natural compost pile, generating its own heat source throughout incubation. Nests containing pieces of green reeds or cattail shoots provide even more heat, being warm to the touch even on a cool, overcast day. This thermal feature is crucial since the chilling of unattended or deserted eggs ranks second only to predation in offspring mortality.

As naturalists reluctantly admit, nature's plan is not always perfect. Over the years of working with loons I have found a handful of nests that wouldn't have met building code requirements. Instead of distinctive mounds, these were little more than slight depressions scratched into the shoreline with the egg or eggs laid literally on the ground. Often these "nests" are found in and under dense shore bushes such as alders or sheep laurel. Because this type of nest site is usually dark, damp and lacking in the internal warmth of the compost pile nests, the incubating loon is forced to spend virtually every minute of the day and night keeping the eggs at an even temperature. The good news is that the surrounding cover vegetation helps camouflage the nesting birds, hiding their presence from predators or human encroachment.

Ironically the most ideal nest site I ever found was the stage for a tragic ending. A foot-high compost mound containing two eggs was located on a floating mat of roots and growing reeds. The loon on the nest was nearly hidden by the yard-high vegetation. It was earmarked for success.

A few days after the discovery of the nest, our area was hit by severe thunderstorms accompanied by high winds. I still don't know why, but I was worried about that particular nest. My fears were justified when I canoed to the site the following morning. Strong winds and waves had tipped the floating island completely over, scattering nest and eggs across the pond bottom. I wonder if loons ever cry.

The perfect nest: constructed of compostable materials, surrounded by water deep enough for submerged escape, commanding a wide view and located in a marsh full of song birds. Who could ask for anything more?

9

Loon country

incubation

Incubation

It is undoubtedly the most traumatic month of the loon's residence in the Adirondacks: incubation. A nesting loon is truly a sitting duck. The black and white plumage stands out in sharp contrast to the greens and blues of foliage and water. Remaining stationary and silent helps shield the loon from most human discovery, but sharp-eyed crows usually know of its presence soon enough. Unattended eggs have little chance in crow country.

What we perceive as silence and solitude in the wilderness is noise and confusion to a nesting loon. Bird calls, insect hums and frog noises are everywhere. Added to these living sounds are the other voices of the wilderness. Creaking trees, rustling foliage and lapping waves create a constant din that has to be dissected and deciphered as normal or threatening. It is a rare moment when nesting loons are completely relaxed. There is also the ever increasing noise of man in loon country. Sounds of boat motors, those of planes flying overhead, and human shouts and laughter simply add to the cacophony.

Both loons share in the incubation process. In extreme cases, one will have the day shift, and the other the night. Generally, four-hour stints are normal. The changing of the guard occurs at the same time (precise enough to set a watch by) each day during the month-long vigil.

Along with the usual unpleasant daily occurrences experienced by the loons such as stinging insects, storms, hot sun and monotony, nature carries some deadly tricks in her bag. One spring during the mid-seventies I concentrated on one attentive nesting pair. It was one of those muggy periods that spawned several intense electrical storms. The island where the nest was located took enough lightning hits to make me leave my blind and seek shelter on the mainland. At last more settled weather moved into the region. The remainder of the incubation was for the most part bluebird weather. Finally the hatch date arrived . . . and went. Thirty-five days passed. This was unheard of. Forty days came and went with no sign of a hatch or the muffled peeping.

On the forty-fourth day, Shar huddled with me in the blind. Finally, at about eleven in the morning the second loon swam close to the nest, and after some loon conversation the nesting bird slowly slid off the nest and joined its mate in the water. Without looking back, they both dove suddenly only to come up far out in the pond. They had left the nest for good. I believe that lightning had killed both eggs. I will never know for sure. On the forty-sixth day the crows came.

A typical island nest site. Because islands are also favorite camping spots, the number of site choices is dwindling rapidly.

Incubation

The first few days of incubation are uneasy ones for the brooding bird. It must be difficult for a water bird to suddenly adapt to living on land.

A photo grouping of nine incubating loons shows a wide variety of nests. They range from sculpted marsh mounds to simple shallow depressions. In 1974, in my study area, the loons on nine nests produced fourteen eggs with ten successful hatches. Only five pairs nested there in 1984. Of the eight eggs laid, three hatched. Man, crows and weather were largely responsible for the losses.

The mere presence of man in loon country is upsetting.

Strong wind has always been the Nemesis of wild creatures. Sounds are distorted and movement is everywhere. Exposed eggs are easily chilled on windy days.

Insects

During incubation the woods hum with a variety of biting insects. The loon is obviously not spared, but it can do little more than shake its head occasionally.

Heat

Because most loon nests are relatively unshaded, the incubating bird receives the full intensity of the sun. Constant panting aids body cooling.

Rain

Warm rains in the Adirondacks are rare; cold fronts often accompany periods of precipitation. The risk of egg chilling is high during rainy days, and I make it a rule to keep my distance in wet weather, especially with skittish nesting birds.

Predators

As all other creatures, loons have their share of natural enemies. Geographic location apparently has a bearing on which is the leading threat. For instance, in the Adirondacks the loons and the chicks are at the mercy of four major predators: man, crows, snapping turtles and raccoons. Yet, in New Hampshire, raccoons come in second only to man as the most dangerous enemy. There, reports of raccoons swimming a quarter mile or more to reach a loon nest and its eggs are not uncommon. In other areas, large fish such as northern pike and muskellunge are a definite threat to young loons. In the Great Lakes, it was small fish, carrying deadly botulism that caused the death of thousands of loons after the unsuspecting birds fed on them. Elsewhere gulls are high on the predator list.

However, there is no question that, no matter where loons are found, man is still the ultimate predator. For years loons were shot for sport. Later man branded the birds as fishing competitors and destroyed them when he could. Egg collectors raided their nests, and fly tiers turned the feathers of this fish eater into fish catchers. Even the Migratory Bird Treaty Act of 1916, and the threat of large fines for violators did little to protect the loons. Killing and maiming with gun

and motorboat had few eye witnesses, especially in the Adirondack back country.

Even as recently as the 1950's, reports of loons being killed in the Adirondacks were common. The "damn fish eater" reputation was still the loon's mill stone. A dead loon meant better fishing. To today's hiking and camping generation, reared on Wild Kingdom, this part of Adirondack history is infuriating. "How could people be so cruel . . . and so stupid?" is the usual response. The mores of one generation usually astound the next. I spent many hours in the Adirondack back country in those years. Thinking back to what was acceptable behavior then makes me shudder now. When the black flies and mosquitoes became unbearable, we sprayed pure DDT on our skin to repel them! Empty bottles and cans were simply held underwater until they sank. Out of sight, out of mind. Nature would clean up after us. If the trout were biting, you kept catching them . . . and catching them. They probably would not bite the next day anyway.

The 1970's brought revolution and revelation to our way of thinking about the world around us. "My God, we're losing a great country!" became the rallying cry. New laws were introduced. Motorboats were outlawed in many remote lakes and ponds. A new morality came to the Adirondacks. Trash and garbage were no longer kicked aside or overboard. The back-to-nature movement also brought a *new* wave of visitors to the back country, people who were not content to bask in the solitude or catch a few fish. The modern lightweight boats and camping gear allowed more and more inexperienced people to explore unspoiled areas, to compete for camping space, to create new spots for tents and latrines. I bitterly remember finding an active island loon nest site commandeered by campers, the abandoned eggs slowly rotting away. I couldn't just paddle away in silence, but I knew I had to control my anger. I calmly called to the campers and pointed out the wasted nest. The spokesman of the group loudly informed me that they were on vacation and had just as much right to camp there as anybody or anything! Man is definitely a predator.

The Ultimate Hardship: Death

Although not directly connected with "nesting hardships," death does occur. I discovered the carcass of this loon on another pair's territory. Decomposition was so advanced, it was impossible to determine the cause of death.

A conservation officer allowed me to photograph, weigh and measure this loon before it was sent away for examination. A necropsy revealed that the loon had been shot.

Incubation Behavior: Changing Shifts

Almost like clockwork, the male and female loons exchange nesting duties at regular intervals during daylight hours. Over the years I have spent several nights in film blinds close to incubating loons, and I'm almost certain they do not change places during darkness.

Rolling the Egg

To insure uniform development and even temperature, the egg is turned at least once every hour.

Calling on the Nest

In my eighteen years of studying and filming loons, I cannot remember more than five or six instances of nesting birds calling. Instead of photographing this loon from my canoe, I waded out in front of the nest. I didn't realize I was blocking the bird's escape route until it wailed at me threateningly.

When a nesting loon senses danger or hears unexplained noises, it instinctively lowers its head and neck. "On alert," as this posture is called, enables the loon to slip quietly off the nest and flee underwater. The lowered head may also help camouflage the bird by covering the startling white breast.

Sleeping on the Nest

A warm afternoon, a quiet pond and a touch of boredom seem to lull an incubating loon to sleep. Most of the time, the mere click of my camera was enough to wake the dozing bird, but not always. One bird in particular nodded off to such a degree that its bill touched the front of the nest before it awoke with a start.

Loon country

hatching

Hatching

One of nature's most perfectly designed containers is the egg. The hard shell is made up of thousands of minute wedge-shaped fragments, much like the curved keystone over a castle door. Although this remarkable construction permits great support of downward pressure, much less exertion is needed from within the egg to break through its wall. An average eggshell measures about seventeen one-thousandths of an inch thick.

Beneath the shell is a leathery sack, the membrane. Because the shell is porous, this waterproof sack keeps unwanted moisture out of the egg. At the same time, it lets normal evaporation occur from within. Inside the membrane is the egg white or albumen. This thick liquid completely surrounds the yolk and the embryo, cushioning them against impact as well as forming a barrier against bacteria attempting to reach the embryo. The yolk is simply a food source for the growing embryo. The larger the yolk, the more developed the hatchling will be. In a robin's egg, the yolk only occupies about one-fifth of the egg's volume, and the chick is hatched blind, featherless and nearly helpless. On the other hand, with many water birds such as ducks, geese and loons, the chick emerges down-covered with open eyes, alert and mobile within an hour after hatching. The yolk in these eggs occupies more than a third of the egg's total volume.

The usual incubation period for a loon egg is twenty-nine days. Forty-eight hours before the actual hatching the chick begins to display sounds and movement. Faint peeping can be heard from as far away as twelve feet. The rudiments of imprinting between the chick and the parent bird occur at this time. Although unhatched, the tiny bird may be able to recognize the rhythm of sounds made by the parents. Movement of the chick is essential to escape from the egg. Slowly, but persistently, the unhatched bird turns end to end, separating the membrane from the shell. Once separation is completed, hatching is possible.

On the twenty-ninth day the miracle of "birth" occurs. Provided with an egg tooth, a sharp horny projection at the tip of the upper beak, the chick rips through the membrane and begins to chip away at the shell. Nature has given the unhatched bird unusually large neck muscles for its task. They shrink back to normal size shortly after hatching, and the egg tooth sloughs off. Jabbing, jabbing, the chick slowly pecks a tiny hole through the outside of the shell letting air in. The chick begins to breathe for the first time. The hole gets larger. The brooding adult, aware of what is happening but helpless to assist until now, slides off the nest just long enough to moisten its body before returning to the egg. Water droplets smeared on the egg act as a softening agent and aid the chick in the breakthrough. The peck hole gets larger and tiny cracks appear. The cracks lengthen and suddenly, with an extra surge, the baby breaks out. A loon chick has hatched!

Bathed in the first rays of sunrise, a hatching chick struggles to break out of the egg. Unless the brooding bird is flushed off the nest, most loon eggs are hatched under the body of the parent. Because the adult bird slipped off the nest momentarily, I was able to get this rare shot.

The newly hatched chick remains hidden under the parent's warm body as it dries out. The adult holds its body slightly off the nest to avoid injuring the chick.

The chick peers out from under a wing, and between yawns, surveys its new world.

The chick's size in relation to the adult's is evident as the baby rests on its parent's large webbed foot.

Uttering soft sounds, the parent inspects the chick, thus continuing the imprinting process. The chick must be made to recognize its parents by sight and sound and be trained to distinguish them from any other bird, animal or object. Its survival depends on it.

Peeping continuously, the young bird explores the nooks and crannies of its parent's body, crawling through the oily feathers. Without realizing it, the chick is waterproofing its downy coat.

The chick makes its way toward the water. Loon intelligence is displayed as the chick elects to back down the incline to the pond's edge.

The chick pauses momentarily, looking out at the pond. Unlike ducklings and goslings which are usually led to water by a parent, loon chicks possess an instinctive attraction for water, often entering it before the adult.

Half crawling, half tumbling, the chick enters the water. It is a giant step for the young bird. Once it leaves the shore, it may be more than three years before it touches solid ground again, and then only to mate and nest.

Waterproofed and bobbing like a fuzzy cork,
the young loon floats alone in the quiet water.
Although not yet five hours old, it is a natural
swimmer.

There is one last task to be performed before the adult loon leaves: the removal of egg shells from the nest. Larger pieces are carried out and dropped in the water; smaller bits are eaten. If egg shells were left in the nest, predators might be attracted. For some reason loons sense the need to protect the nest site even though they may never return to it.

The adult and chick move to open water.

Imprinting continues as the chick learns to recognize its parent on the water. Identification by sight, both three dimensional and in silhouette form, is crucial, but scent is not a factor. Loons, like most birds, have very little sense of smell or taste.

The loon family together for the first time.

underwater

Filming the Loon Underwater: The Impossible Dream

From the time I saw my first loon the mystery of what this diving bird did in its underwater world intrigued me. I had, in a few rare instances, caught a fleeting glimpse of a submerged loon as it streaked under my canoe. The image was indistinct, and it appeared yellow and gray when viewed through the pond water. The dream of actually filming a loon underwater became an obsession. To our knowledge it had never been done in the natural state. Thus, the answer to how it could be accomplished was unknown. Shar and I listed the stumbling blocks. If the shy birds would rarely tolerate the approach of humans either on their nest or in the middle of a pond, how could we expect to get close enough to film them underwater? What about their speed and agility while diving? It was unlikely that a diver could overtake a fleeing loon underwater. Another hurdle concerned their reaction to having a human invade their underwater domain. We knew that the presence of an otter, probably the only land animal comparable in swimming ability, evoked a frenzied reaction from the loons. We had to think of something that would keep the loons from leaving the area. Since beginning my filming I had been able to get the best close-up shots when a newly hatched chick was present. Would a chick on the scene keep the adults close underwater, too? It was worth a try.

Since I had no experience in diving, our next quest was to find an adventurous soul who was proficient at both scuba diving and underwater cinematography. Someone suggested we contact Doug Warner. I had met Doug a few years before and I knew his reputation. Every town has a Doug Warner. Although shy and unassuming, he was branded a wild kid early in life. Able to build or repair almost anything, Doug always owned the fastest cars, motorcycles and boats. He was a natural athlete, but shunned organized sports, preferring to spend his time hunting, fishing and skiing. Only ten minutes with Doug convinced us we had found the right man. He was an expert scuba diver and we were offering him the one thing he lived for: a challenge. He accepted it. There was only one problem. He had very little experience with any camera, let alone a bulky 16mm movie camera in an underwater housing. Underwater photography was a new area for us as well. With the naive enthusiasm of doing what had never been done before,

we began laying the groundwork for our project.

Using funds provided by the National Wildlife Federation, we purchased an expensive underwater camera housing. With the equipment spread out on the garage floor, Shar and Doug agonized over instruction manuals and slowly mastered the techniques necessary to assemble the housing, insert the camera, adjust the settings and see to the host of details involved in underwater filming. My contribution was of another kind. I had to select the right loon pair, with a newly hatched chick or chicks. Their pond should be pristine clear. A tall order. Having worked with many loon pairs over the preceding two years, I felt I knew their personalities fairly well. Some pairs were immediately eliminated as they were too skittish when encountering humans, especially when raising their chicks. Others were eliminated because the water clarity in their ponds was poor. We finally decided on one pair I had affectionately named Fat and Skinny. Both birds were accustomed to my presence, and I knew from previous experience that Fat was, in comparison to other loons, quite aggressive. The previous year he had slammed into the bow of my canoe, soaking my equipment, after I had paddled too close to their five-day-old chick. Doug simply smiled when I described the incident. Unfortunately, the pond Fat and Skinny called home was less than ideal in water clarity, but it would have to do. The other two factors, a successful hatch and sunny weather were in God's hands.

The days of late June found us still working on the technical and logistic aspects of our project. When we water-tested the camera and housing in a nearby pond, we discovered that the housing had been designed for salt water use and would not attain neutral buoyancy in fresh water. It sank to the bottom. Back to the drawing board. Several layers of styrofoam taped to the underside of the housing overcame the buoyancy problem, but the tape came loose seconds after immersion. More head-scratching. After experimenting with various tapes, we finally found that the freezer variety would work. Scuba equipment was also checked and double checked and the tank filled. A supply of special high-speed film was stored in our refrigerator. We had contacted our film laboratory in New York City, and they agreed to give us preferential service by processing and returning our footage imme-

diately. We hoped we hadn't missed any details.

On the last day of the month I checked the nesting loons. When Skinny raised up to turn the eggs, I could detect faint peeping. It wouldn't be long. That evening, as usual, the conversation centered on our impossible dream. Now that the preparations were finished and a loon hatch was imminent, the moral aspect of the project surfaced. We had to weigh scientific importance, aesthetic satisfaction and personal pride in doing what had never been done against the possibility of harming the loons. The three of us agreed that if the loons or their offspring were being endangered, we would scrap the project. On July 2nd a single loon hatched. The second egg, apparently infertile, was discarded. The remaining chick seemed healthy and alert, and ideal weather was forecast for the following day. We were ready!

Day One—July 3, 1971

The morning following the hatch found us on a small island in Fat and Skinny's pond. Since we were filming with natural lighting, we had to wait until the sun was high enough. We had located the new loon family shortly after we arrived on the pond, and we could see them from the island. The sun was climbing. This was it. After checking our equipment in the canoe one last time, Shar and I boarded as Doug waded a few yards out from shore. As we backed toward him, he grasped the stern and we slowly towed him toward the loons.

Loud distress calls filled the air as we neared the birds, and they reached even higher intensity as I lifted the camera housing over the side to our diver. In an eruption of bubbles Doug sank beneath the surface and started toward the loons. Suddenly all hell broke loose! Skinny left the chick and, screaming wildly, churned upright in a zig-zag path around our canoe. Fat had more drastic plans! Crash diving, he streaked by Doug, missing his head by inches. Executing a high-speed turn, Fat made another lunge. Shar and I sat frozen in the canoe. We weren't expecting anything like this! As Doug thrashed around in the muddied water, Fat attacked again and again. Then Doug's air bubbles stopped. So did our hearts. I was scrambling over the side when Doug surfaced, huffing and puffing. He thrust the camera housing to Shar, grabbed the canoe, and we paddled furiously to the nearest shore. He too had been totally unprepared for

Fat's attacks. After the first few seconds of filming, the camera jammed. Shaking it vigorously, Doug got it running again, but by that time Fat was on him. All Doug could do to protect himself was to use the camera housing as a shield to ward off the attacks. Yet, he kept filming. The water had become so riled by the activity that Doug could see nothing. He decided to hold his breath, hoping that would allow him better visibility. Now we knew why his air bubbles had stopped. Doug casually admitted he had some trouble breathing. Who wouldn't?

We returned to the island. I was convinced that we should give up the project. Our initial concern had been for the safety of the loons, but in one four-minute session the tables had turned. Now we were worried about Doug's welfare. He said he would respect majority rule, but felt that we should try at least one more dive to use up the remaining film in the camera. He also hoped that by working with the loons in deeper water, bottom mud would not be so apt to impair visibility. We ate lunch, rested, and after lengthy discussion, towed our gutsy diver out to the field of battle.

As Doug submerged we could see that he was once again going to have his hands full. Fat torpedoed toward him, and from the surface it looked as if the determined loon was driving his bill right at Doug's yellow air tank. The deeper water enabled our diver to maneuver more easily, and he met each attack with the running movie camera. It was finally Fat who gave up. Doug was just too persistent. Surfacing, the large loon swam over to Skinny and the chick, and they sat there quietly in the water. This enabled Doug to get as close as seven or eight feet from them. Careful not to make any sudden moves to incite another attack, Doug kept the camera going until the film ran out. Silently, but swiftly, we moved the canoe between him and the loons allowing Doug to hitch a ride back to the island. Once again he complained about breathing problems while submerged, but after checking the scuba equipment carefully, he finally came to the unlikely conclusion that he must be running low on air. Getting the tank refilled meant having to make a nine-mile trip to town and back. By that time we would have lost the best of the afternoon sun. In addition, we needed time to rethink our tactics to see if there was a better way. We had gotten one roll of film

(about three minutes on the screen), and we didn't even know if that was usable. We agreed to begin again the next morning.

Day Two—July 4, 1971

Doug arrived with additional support: his wife and his rowboat. He explained that he had not run out of air the day before, but that a faulty regulator caused his breathing difficulties. He had borrowed another regulator. I stayed on the island with the equipment while the others went off to find the loons. A long circle of the pond was necessary before they located Skinny and the baby. Then they had to return to the island. We finally loaded both boats and headed out. It was much easier for Doug to ride out in the rowboat and go over the side than to be towed behind the canoe. Skinny went into her now familiar dance routine while Doug concentrated on filming the chick. It was amazing! The baby loon at three days old dove down fifteen feet! Tiny beads of water clung to its gray-black down, making it look silver under the water. At one point, to our astonishment, the chick nestled on Doug's shoulder.

To dive, the baby paddled furiously, nearly straight down, using its oversized feet and stubby wings. Then it stopped, relaxed completely, and popped to the surface like a cork. Then Fat arrived. Skinny escorted the chick away while Fat kept Doug busy. Apparently Fat had forgotten about his experience with Doug the day before, since he attacked just as vigorously as the first time. We decided to take a break.

Around 1:30 we began again. The wind had picked up, and the paddling was harder. We found the adult loons, but the baby was nowhere in sight. We sat along shore in the boats assuming that the adults had hidden the baby somewhere in the sheep laurel nearby. Quite by chance, Shar spotted the chick only a few feet away, hugging the shoreline. We held a conference. Doug wanted to film the baby without having to contend with Fat. We agreed to leave Doug hidden near the shore and allow the adult loons to decoy us in the boats down the pond away from the baby. After all, birds can't count, and they would never know that we had left Doug behind.

We moved into action and Fat and Skinny cooperated. We followed them all the way down the pond chatting happily about the great foot-

age Doug must be getting. We were about five hundred yards from Doug and the baby, when the loons abruptly, with a short run, took to the air and headed straight back for the baby . . . and Doug! We were too far away to warn him. We paddled frantically, yelling as loudly as we could. We felt sure Doug couldn't hear us from his underwater location. We went so far as to bang paddles and oars against the boats hoping *that* sound would carry. Fat landed and immediately dove on Doug. We learned later that Fat came at Doug from behind, hitting his flippers and causing him to somersault in the water. Fat circled and returned, dodged the camera housing, and rammed his bill into Doug's forehead! When we finally got to him, Doug was surfacing, blood trickling down his face. We were stunned, but Doug merely announced with a grin, "Hey Kip! A loon just bit me." Enough was enough.

Day Three—July 5, 1971

It was hazy despite a strong wind. We loaded the camera and set out. Skinny was alone with the chick, and Doug, shooting from both underwater and surface levels, used nearly a roll of film. Skinny had almost found her courage. She rushed at Doug, but pulled up short just before she hit him. Then she returned to her more comfortable runs and dances. Fat arrived just as the film ran out. It didn't take much convincing to get Doug back into the boat while I changed the film.

Although we still had adequate lighting, the wind was increasing in intensity. A look to the west showed a storm front moving in. Our time was running out. Waves were slamming against the boats as Doug plunged in. I quickly handed him the camera and he submerged. Fat lost no time. He left Skinny and the baby and diving straight for Doug, hit the camera housing. The water was so turbulent that Doug and Fat couldn't find each other most of the time. We hauled Doug into the boat and fought the high seas back to land. I think now that God and Mother Nature were trying to tell us something. Had we continued, Doug or the loons might have been seriously injured. Yet we had done the impossible. We had gotten films of loons underwater in the wild! All that was left was the agony of waiting: getting the 400 feet of film processed and seeing how much had actually been captured on film.

The Dive

With an expulsion of air, a compression of feathers and a powerful thrust of its oversized feet, a loon executes a typical "crash dive."

The Rare

Photos/Doug Warner

Captured on movie film in its underwater world, a loon displays its normal method of locomotion. Unlike a diving duck's, the loon's legs and feet are held laterally to the body for nearly perfect leverage. When not chasing fish or escaping danger, submerged loons often poke along pond bottoms, overturning rocks and debris in search of food.

The Rarest

A loon's use of its wings underwater is a very unusual occurrence. Most naturalists claim it is not done at all. To film it was extremely rare, and these may be the only such photographs of this kind. As a rule, loons seldom use a wing or wings underwater. To make a high-speed turn, either in pursuit of fish or in an emergency situation, the bird may suddenly extend a wing. The partially opened wings seem to act as brakes and help to lift the bird up and over obstacles, in this case, our cameraman.

All of my "underwater" loon filming is now done from my canoe. After locating a submerged bird, I just hold a waterproof 35mm camera under water and click away. It is "wing shooting" at best, but occasionally luck is with me, as evidenced by the photograph above.

Underwater: One year later

Photo/Sharon Taylor

Based upon our experiences the year before, we approached our underwater filming as experts. We knew now what to expect, and Fat and Skinny had returned after their winter migration. This time we would be prepared. I bought scuba gear for myself, and Doug gave me some lessons. I can't say I felt comfortable with diving, but I desperately wanted slides as well as movies of loons underwater. During the early spring, we designed makeshift headgear to protect us from Fat's attacks. We used a wire basket, a plastic laundry basket, and various strappings to hold them in place. When the day arrived, we enlisted the help of another friend, Murray Latham, and we used one rowboat and one canoe. When we donned our wet suits and headgear, we looked like creatures from outer space, and our spirits were as high.

Murray rowed the boat carrying Doug and me. Shar was alone in the canoe. We located the loon family in a quiet bay that seemed ideal for our purposes. Doug and I went in. Murray kept the rescue craft close, just in case. Nothing happened. That is to say, Fat did nothing. Skinny was true to form, doing her runs and dances and screaming the whole time. Fat acted unconcerned. He wouldn't dive or even come toward us. He just sat there with the baby. Doug and I surfaced, and we tried to think of something that would make Fat dive. Nothing seemed to work, so we discarded our protective headgear, and went under again, even closer to the baby.

On the surface, Shar was sitting in our somewhat leaky wood and canvas canoe. At one point, she drifted quite close to the loons and, on a whim, scooped the chick right out from under Fat's bill. She put the chick behind her in the canoe where it bobbed happily in the water which had leaked in. The baby called out its normal "peep peep peep", and Fat looked all around trying to find it. He finally approached the canoe and arched his neck over the side just inches from Shar. Then he turned and swam a few feet away.

Doug and I came up. When we heard what had happened, we decided that if Fat didn't react to *that,* he wouldn't react to anything. Shar carefully put the chick back in the water, and it rejoined Fat as if nothing had happened. Then Shar started thinking about what she had done. What possessed her to challenge Fat like that knowing what he had done to Doug the year before? She suddenly realized how threatening Fat's long bill had looked when he peered into the canoe. We had all been lucky. We debated which of Fat's actions were normal: those in 1971, or those in 1972? In any case, they were twice-in-a-lifetime experiences. We have never again tried to duplicate them.

12

Loon country

raising the young loon

Raising the Young Loon

Rearing the chick is a full-time, seemingly thankless job. Until the young bird is nearly capable of flight, it is a raspy-voiced eating machine. The chick, especially during the first month, is also the epitome of a spoiled only child. Constantly calling to the parent birds for food and pecking at their faces and bodies, it often drops what they put in its bill. Patiently, the adults dive to retrieve the morsel and try again. Young loons are fed a variety of things, including pond vegetation, leeches and freshly killed small fish.

The learning process seems to begin about the fourth week. The adults continue to gather food, but stop placing it in the baby's bill. Instead, they drop it in front of the chick, forcing it to either snatch the food quickly or to have to dive to get it. The next step in the training program is to release small live fish near the young loon to encourage the response of chase and capture. The chick seems to learn quickly although a streak of stubbornness is sometimes displayed. Occasionally the young bird will refuse to retrieve the released fish, preferring to nip at the face of the nearest parent bird and whine in an irritating voice. The adults ultimately cure their offspring of these temper tantrums by recatching the fish and eating them in front of the youngster. The point is obviously well made for the growing bird soon learns to work for its food or go hungry.

In the Adirondacks, the loons tend to feed their offspring pond vegetation for a much longer period of time than is reported in other loon habitats. This is due to the scarcity of fingerlings and minnows, fish the chick can swallow. In many of our Adirondack ponds the competition for small food fish is fierce. Kingfishers, ospreys and gulls patrol from above; herons and bitterns wade the shores and shallow areas, as do raccoons and mink; fish-eating ducks, otters and loons work the deeper water; and large fish also take their share. The introduction of salmon, hybrid brook trout and fast-growing splake has added more voracious mouths to feed. Brown trout cruise the warmer parts of some of these waters, and lake trout hunt the colder depths. The life expectancy for a minnow in that kind of neighborhood is short!

The Chick: The First Two Weeks

Up until its third week, the infant chick swims a precarious line between safety and danger. The parent birds provide mobile protection platforms: their own bodies. During cool or rainy periods or after the chick has spent an extended time in the water, an adult will encourage the youngster to climb up under a wing or on its back. This provides both warmth and protection from predators.

The growing chick is fed almost hourly. It has been estimated that the young bird, during its first few weeks, consumes thirty percent of its body weight daily. Pond vegetation makes up a large amount of its diet. As shown here, one of the adults with a bill full of underwater aquatic plants encourages the chick to peck small morsels.

The chick at fourteen days is showing signs of color change. This first molt causes the soft, gray-black down to be replaced by a reddish, coarser coat.

During its fourth week the chick's molt is nearly completed, and rapid growth is evident.

The young bird, though pampered and protected by its parents, begins to show signs of adult behavior such as wing flaps and foot waggles.

The young bird continuously begs for food. Although well into the sixth week, the parent birds still provide about one-third of the chick's diet.

A loon, carrying a brook trout, heads across its pond to feed the chick. Pond vegetation and fish are brought to the surface much more frequently during chick rearing.

During darkness the loon family probably feeds on shallow pond vegetation such as water lily stems or floating pond weeds.

Nearing its second month, the chick is left alone for longer periods, especially in areas where little human activity is evident. On the more heavily traveled canoe routes, one parent usually accompanies the youngster.

Having undergone another molt, the growing youngster shows faint adult markings on its back.

13

Loon country

congregation

Congregation

Midsummer brings about a behavioral change among loons. Normally anti-social by nature, they now welcome other loons into their territories. Even before the sun is fully up, the first visitors appear in the sky. Though the territorial barriers are down, a shred of loon etiquette is maintained. Each bird calls loudly as it circles the pond as if asking permission to come in for a landing. Usually, one of the resident pair will answer with a short "whoop." Apparently, permission has been granted.

Within an hour, as many as six or seven loons will have gathered. In this convention of hermits, nervous excitement is evident. Almost giddy in behavior, the members of the feathered flotilla yelp and whoop and jostle one another as they tour the pond. Each bird seems intent on inciting the group. Sudden wing-flapping and bill-dipping inspire the others into ecstatic frenzy. Often, two or three loons abruptly raise their bodies out of the water, and breasts thrown forward, wings and neck back, run for several yards before splashing down in torrents of spray. If one loon dives, the entire group follows. Several seconds may pass before they surface in small groups of three or four. Then, like adults caught playing a children's game, the loons settle back into the water and continue touring the pond in prim and proper fashion. A midmorning wind usually brings a halt to the loon reunion. Singly or in pairs, the visiting birds leave.

Exactly why loons congregate is not known. Perhaps it is a prelude to migration. In any case it is an exciting time both for the loons and for me.

Variations of the penguin walk are displayed when these introverted birds gather. Because the loons remind her of athletes in competition, Shar calls these antics the "Loon Olympics."

14

Loon country

the juvenile

The Juvenile

At ten weeks the young loon becomes a juvenile. Because of its rapid growth rate and emerging feathers, the juvenile spends much of its time attending to its new coat; preening is constant. It begins to acquire the coloration and markings of an adult. The pattern on the body is muted, but stripes and squares are visible. Though the body markings are present, there is no evidence of either collar or necklace.

The juvenile is almost as large as the adults. It is now able to feed itself and is frequently left alone for long periods of time. However, when a parent is present, the young bird occasionally reverts to its childhood behavior and pecks at the parent, begging for food. It still has its crackling, rasping voice, which only a mother could love.

Normally only one parent is present to watch over the offspring through the late summer and fall. The other parent has left the pond. It may have started its migratory flight early, or may be spending its time on a nearby lake. The remaining parent does not stay as close as it did in the early summer, but nevertheless seems to know the juvenile's location at all times, and is invariably there in case of emergency. The adult still wails on occasion when intruders go near the young bird. It is almost comical to hear the parent bird "warning" the occupants of a boat who have ventured too close, especially when the juvenile appears to be perfectly capable of fending for itself.

Sporting its new plumage, the juvenile loon paddles slowly across its territorial waters. The young bird will probably not acquire adult plumage until its third year.

A slow stretching exercise reveals the size and feather development of the twelve-week old loon.

Although still considered a ''growing chick,'' the young bird possesses excellent hearing and eyesight. A strong and agile swimmer, it is no longer threatened by predators such as large fish or snapping turtles. With the possible exception of eagles, most avian flesh-eaters are ignored.

Family bonds are not easily severed. Although forced to be alone most of the time, the juvenile is occasionally allowed to join a parent bird for short periods to fish, preen or visit.

The Juvenile Loon Flying

The young loon's first inclination toward flying is to battle the water as if it were to blame for holding him down. It is early October. An urgency seems to dominate the young bird's mind as he flaps his wings, rolls over on his back, and slaps the surface, his wings sending sprays of water high into the air.

As the days pass, he finally learns to move across the pond surface using his wings as oars. Though it makes the young bird travel faster, it does nothing to lift him into the air. There are more days of practice. A new technique is needed. With flapping wings, he now tries running across the water, each run becoming longer. The young loon is able, after repeated runs, to raise his breast out of the water, but he can't lift his feet and tail. Even more practice is necessary. And then, one windy morning . . .

Flapping its wings, the juvenile faces the wind in preparation for a flight attempt.

The magic moment arrives. The juvenile loon lifts off the water to begin its first successful flight.

Although finally airborne, the young loon will need many more days of practice flights before it can begin its migratory journey.

15

autumn changes

Autumn Changes

Autumn comes quickly to the Adirondacks and the black and white loons suddenly find themselves in a technicolor world. It is not only the leaves and plants that are changing from a summer coat; the loons are also undergoing a change. Their winter plumage is emerging. Feathers floating on the pond can be seen more frequently.

This changing of coats, or postnuptial molt, is gradual, and it varies in degree of intensity from loon to loon. The base of the bill and upper neck are the first to show gray patches. The molt extends downward during the days and weeks. Although nature has signaled the change while the birds are still on their summer range, full molting does not occur until the loons have finished their migration. A premature shedding of wing feathers could hinder or even prevent the loon from flying. It is believed that some birds are flightless on their winter range. Autumn changes are far reaching.

*Experiencing its first autumn, the juvenile
loon cruises a multi-colored shoreline.*

For reasons unknown, certain loons molt more quickly than others. This bird, in late October, has lost nearly all of its summer plumage and, except for a black bill tip, almost resembles a juvenile.

16

departure

Departure

For many of the bird species found in the Adirondacks, especially the insect eaters, migration begins as early as August. Although length of daylight and weather are factors, a declining food supply is the primary reason they head south. September and October find the plant and seed eaters also departing. Aside from the resident birds, usually only the fish eaters remain into November. The loons are among the last to leave. With their thick waterproof plumage, cold temperatures and north winds do not seem to bother them. Ice-in is the trap they have to avoid. Some don't. Late hatching juveniles who are still unable to fly can only await a slow death. Injured adults whose flying is impaired can expect the same fate. Deadlines have to be met in nature.

As usual, loons do not all follow the same blueprint. September departure of single birds or pairs is not uncommon. I do not think that these birds head directly back to their ocean habitat; they probably hop-scotch from lake to lake on a slow southern route. In any case, our Adirondack loons depart much the same as they arrive in early spring, with little fanfare.

Its mate having departed the pond weeks earlier and its offspring capable of flight, the remaining bird is free to leave. Bathed in an early morning sun, it circles its territorial waters one last time before heading southward.

epilogue

Epilogue: Loons and People

For a number of years I believed that loons and people could not coexist. I thought that if man moved into a loon habitat the loons would move out. Well, fortunately for the loons, I was wrong. In fact, loons seem to adapt quite well to the presence of people as long as the birds are not harassed or their nest sites disturbed.

It is much more difficult for *me* to adjust to the influx of people. I keep comparing the old days to what is happening now. When I began filming loons, few people used the back country. It was not unusual to hike five miles or more to a remote pond, only to turn around and walk out because there was another boat already there. We considered *that* crowded. In 1965, Shar and I, just married, enjoyed almost three months honeymooning in my favorite wilderness region. From mid-June to the first week in September we saw only nine other people.

In those years the "mind-your-own-business" attitude was so strong it sometimes bordered on the humorous. One summer early in my filming, I was babysitting a loon nest on a small island. I was determined to get aerial shots of the loons on and around the nest, but couldn't afford to charter a plane. My solution was to take a 36-foot extension ladder to the island. I'm glad nobody saw me tie the ladder across my canoe. Once I reached the island, I extended the ladder and, with considerable effort, leaned it up against a tall birch. I climbed up with all my photo gear and tied the ladder and myself to the tree. What a view! While I was waiting for the loon to return to the nest, two old-timers in a rowboat came around the end of the island. As they trolled by, one of them looked up and saw me. He said to his fishing buddy, "There's a guy up in that tree over there." The other man looked up and nodded to me. I nodded back, and they went on their way, never missing a stroke with the oars.

In the early 1970's new laws governing the use of state and private lands in the Adirondacks were passed. When the dust settled, we found that the new maps now labeled our honeymoon and loon territory: "Canoe Area." Unintentionally, a monster had been created. Outsiders saw the maps and apparently thought that this was the only place to come for canoe trips. Although "discovery" of the canoe area began slowly, that was to change. In 1975, approximately 4300 campers and canoeists signed the register before paddling and portaging into this once pristine area. The word spread. The ice-free season of 1985 found 8700 names in the registry, and those who didn't bother to sign in were estimated at an additional 2500!

During the course of one day in the summer of 1985, I counted sixty-two boats crossing a 150 acre pond where a loon family lived. Unfortunately, all but three boats detoured from their course to get a closer look at the loon family. The birds themselves invited intrusions because of their instinctive habit of voicing distress calls when a boat is sighted. Multiply this by fifty-nine boats, and one wonders if the loons are not hoarse by day's end. I'm sure none of these wilderness travelers intended to disturb the birds, but often that closer look or one more picture is just as harmful.

An adult loon pair can certainly fend for itself and simply escape all of the human attention by diving or swimming to another part of the pond. The presence of a chick is another matter, especially if the offspring is less than a month old. At this age the young loon is unable to swim rapidly, and it requires frequent feedings. It also needs rest and warmth, which it finds by riding on a parent's back or under its wing. Left undisturbed, the loon family usually seeks a quiet spot and moves slowly allowing the chick to keep up without exhausting itself. When boats approach, their serenity is interrupted. The adults react by running, calling and dancing, in an attempt to divert attention from the baby. The chick, instinctively trying to stay close to its parents, paddles back and forth and in circles, heading first toward one and then the other. It can tire very quickly at this rate. One boat a day would not be a problem, but, fifty-nine?

It is more than the numbers of people that create the problem. We as a people must learn to accept and appreciate the wilderness on its own terms. Most of today's back country visitors come to enjoy the peace and tranquillity of an area, and they only have a few days or a week in which to accomplish it. At home, they are exposed to nature's exciting moments by movies and television, but they tend to forget that what they see in a half-hour show may have taken months or years to photograph or even to occur naturally. Many lack patience, and in trying to see or do something special, inflict unintentional harm on the wildlife and the area. Most mean well, but some seem to have difficulty reconciling their quest for peace and tranquillity with their desire for a dramatic experience.

One year I was watching two islands that are separated only by a narrow waterway. I was sure the loons would nest on one or the other of the islands, and I had four or five potential nest sites staked out. I had spent the morning hurriedly constructing a makeshift blind at each location. In one treeless spot on the larger island I had dug a small foxhole uphill from the shoreline. Other sites were prepared by merely stretching wire between two trees to hang my camouflage. Shortly after noon I settled down in my observation blind on the small island to wait for the loons, never dreaming my preparations would be noticed, much less so totally misinterpreted.

Suddenly around the point came a man, woman and teenage boy who proceeded to beach their canoe at the big island. Even though they were standing close together, they shouted. "Look. Someone's been here! Trapping's not allowed here, is it? Look over there. He's set snares (my wires) for animals! Hey! Here's a pit trap! There's his shovel. Let's break the handle, or maybe we should just take it with us!" They discovered a burned standing tree that had been scorched years ago by an out-of-control campfire. "He's burning trees!" Then the woman found a piece of old weathered board, and using charcoal from the campfire, she wrote a message to me: DO NOT CUT OR BURN TREES! Suddenly the teenager spotted my observation blind. "Hey! There's his tent! Let's go tear it down!"

It was as if they had found a cause: the wrong they had been seeking to set right. With a great sense of purpose, they jumped into their canoe and crossed toward me. I waited until they were almost ashore, then said calmly, "Would you mind waiting until I get out of here before you tear my 'tent' down?" Granted, I was mad at their intrusion, but they didn't wait around for an explanation. Shock, and then embarrassment were followed by panic. Elbows were flying and canoe paddles were going in all directions, splashing water, but making no headway. They couldn't get away fast enough. I wondered if this bit of excitement made their day. It sure ruined mine!

Every now and then I encounter an individual or even a group who renews my optimism in mankind. One day, working the same pond with the parade of people, I saw a group of five canoes coming down the pond. The loon family, as usual, began calling. The occupants of the lead canoe began to change course toward the birds when a loud, bass voice from the last boat said, "Jeff, just leave the loons alone. They're not bothering us, and we're not going to bother them." Jeff got the message. I almost stood up in my blind and applauded.

The writing of this book has forced me to think seriously about my motives and the things we did to get the photographs that you have seen. In the early years we didn't know much about loons. Neither did anyone else. We had no experience or studies to draw upon. Every close-up I got was a first, not only for me, but for the viewing public. Yet I never did anything without considering its possible effect on the loons. We took chances in filming the loons underwater, since we had no idea how they would react, but because the loons meant more to me than the film, they fared better than we did. Few can afford the luxury of spending eighteen years to cover a subject in nature. It was my choice to do it this way.

I spent the summer of 1987 completing certain photo segments of this book. Shar and I traveled one weekend to a pond that usually had a successful loon hatch. We were delighted to find the adults with twin babies, and the old excitement returned. Shar paddled while I focused on one adult that was dancing and vocalizing to lure us away from the chicks. Then something strange happened. Almost simultaneously, Shar stopped paddling and I stopped filming. We looked at each other and knew it was time to leave. We didn't need those pictures; the loons did need to be left alone.

I am often asked about the future of the loons in our area of the Adirondacks. I *know* their numbers are declining, at least in wilderness areas set aside for boating, camping and recreational use. The encroachment of man has reached almost out-of-control proportions. The pounding of feet and pounding of tent stakes are taking their toll. Soil on some portages has been worn so thin that tree root networks are exposed. Campsites are devoid of firewood and ground vegetation. Rainfalls leave large mud stains in the usually clear water in front of almost every camping spot.

The number of wild residents of these areas has dwindled, except for the scavengers. Crows seem to be everywhere and gulls, rarely seen in the Adirondacks twenty years ago, now spend their summers on nearly all of these remote ponds. What of the remaining loons? They probably do get used to humans crisscrossing their territories. The loon chicks can be hidden along shorelines or led to unoccupied parts of their ponds. They are adapting, somewhat. These are minor problems. The major problem is nesting. When the nest sites are gone, the loons will leave. It is as sad and simple as that.

In other areas of the country frequented by loons, help has taken the form of the construction of artificial nesting platforms. As far as I know, this has not been tried in the Adirondacks, nor can it be since the "Forever Wild" clause in our state constitution prohibits man-made structures, even if they are to be used to help preserve wildlife. Thus the provision intended to maintain a "natural" setting allows for human intrusion into an area, but it appears to be driving out at least one form of the "natural" setting, the loon. And the same provision prohibits artificial nesting platforms. Quite an irony. The people will have to decide if they are willing to make some sacrifices to save the nesting areas and therefore, the loons themselves. Would the public tolerate making islands and marshes, which are natural nesting places for several species of birds "off-limits" from mid-May through mid-July? In over-used areas would they consider day trips only, giving the region a well-needed rest? This would let the sores heal and allow new growth to flourish. It would also let the wild creatures return and give those that are there a chance to propagate and lead the kind of lives they once knew.

I would like to leave you with two suggestions to follow when visiting loon country: First, if you're going to take a camera, use it for scenic shots. For a close look at wildlife, choose instead, a good pair of binoculars. You will be able to observe from a distance, without disturbing anything. The second suggestion concerns camping. Everyone seems to love an island campsite, and if this is your choice, take a few minutes to paddle completely around the island at about twenty feet out. Check for active nests of any kind, and if you spot any, please look for another place to camp. You may just save a life or two. The loons and I would like that. The only thing lonelier than the call of a loon . . . is no call at all!

Acknowledgments

A very special thank you goes to Betty Cook whose "gentler, kinder" inspiration gave us the impetus to move forward with this book.

To the hundreds of folks who bet on an unsure thing . . . and bought copies of LOON before it was even published, I thank you for having faith in us.

Another heartfelt thank you goes to Bob and Kathryn Jones. This couple's artistic talents keep me humble. I'm proud to be their friend.

For their helpful attitudes and information, I wish to extend grateful thanks to:

Dr. Michael Kudish, Paul Smith's College of Arts and Sciences
Joseph Rupp, New York State Department of Environmental
    Conservation
Phil Johnstone, New York State Department of Environmental
    Conservation
Meg and Manny Bernstein
AuSableClub, St. Huberts, New York
National Wildlife Federation, Washington, DC

For occasionally making me put down my camera gear and reach for my tackle box and spinning rod, I want to thank my old college roommate and close friend, Jim Flanagan.

Most of all, I thank the loons of the Adirondacks.